Musings

Jill Cote

BookLeaf
Publishing

Presentation by *BookLeaf Publishing*

Web: www.bookleafpub.com

E-mail: info@bookleafpub.com

ISBN: 9789357440912

First edition 2023

I'd like to dedicate this book to my family and friends. They are the people who believe in me, who give me unconditional support and love, who cry with me, who cheer me on. Josh, Bella, Mike, Matt, Mom, Dad, Jen and more. You know who you are.

Open Wounds

Wounds on the skin are easy to see,
They zig-zag across my body in patterns
That tell a story of life and love and loss

Chicken pox scars dot my face,
in my hairline, under my eye, on my chin
Scar on my finger, I sliced it with a gravy bowl
on Thanksgiving

These scars are mark the passage of time,
Of lonely years and long dried tears
Moments that I remember when I see them

Wounds on my heart are hidden,
Wounds that do not heal, that lie open and
bleeding
They are the wounds of deep pain

Losing you is an open wound,
One who cannot knit itself together
Every day there is a reminder and it brings pain

Your smile, your rich accent,
The ways in which you made me feel safe and
loved
Friendship that withstood time and distance

Your death is an open wound,
One that does not fade or heal
Grief hits in the weirdest moments

When I am driving by the Cumbies,
And think of you calling the cashiers "Flower"
Or watching a soccer (football) game

When I am sad or scared,
I expect to hear your voice
"Are you going to be alright?"

A wound deep in my heart,
One that does not knit together
One who whispers in my ear "he's gone"

Should I Reconsider?

I make up my mind quickly,
Yes, no, never in a million years,
Absolutely, without a doubt.

You break my heart…
You are cut off, out.
I will not look back as I leave.

Your choices endanger my family,
I will end our relationship without
A backward glance.

You lie about me….
That's fine, I know the truth,
you will never be my friend.

Should I reconsider my choices?
No, never.
I believe in myself.

I believe in the power of truth,
In the actions we take
And the choices we make.

I believe I make good choices,
I believe in my actions
I believe I am a good person.

I choose love,
I choose family and friends,
I choose to be grateful for my life.

Should I reconsider?
No, never.

The Hardest Part

The hardest part of losing you
is letting you go,
to know I will never again see your face
or hear your voice.

The phone call I received
cut me to my core,
how could you be gone?
We'd only spoken two nights before.

I carry your photos with me
in my backpack every day,
reminding me of simpler times
of happiness and laughter we shared.

The hardest part of losing you
is never hearing your voice,
is only having memories
of thirty years of friendship.

The hardest part of letting go
is knowing you will not be there,
when my kids get married,
when your kids get married.

The hardest part of losing you
is knowing I could have helped,
could have pushed you harder to move,
could have demanded you leave.

The hardest part of losing you
is still loving you with all my heart,
you were one of my best friends,
and that hole will never be filled.

The hardest part of losing you
is the emptiness left behind,
the years stretch out before me
without you.

Things I Love

Hearing rain fall softly on the camper roof,
A gentle drumming in the nighttime silence.
The smell of campfire,
Encircling you in its warm embrace, gently and woodsy.

The stillness of a snowfall,
When then only sound is your breathing,
Soft white powder covers everything,
A blanket over the town.

The smell of anything baking,
Gooey chocolate chip cookies,
The annual Christmas cookies,
Even a Sunday dinner during football season.

READING
The smell of an old well-loved classic,
The feel of the pages between my fingers,
    Words that call me to their pages.

    Music fills my head
    Albums on the record player
    Enjoying 80's music and more,
    Feeling the beat as I do my chores
    Makes the housework a little easier.

Teaching,
Knowing that I am passionate about my subject,
Sharing mythology with my students
Seeing faces alight with understanding
Gives me a great deal of joy

Being a friend
Someone to listen
Someone to lean on
Always here to help when I can,
Makes me feel useful and alive.

Daughter-
Taking care of mom and dad,
Helping out in any way I can
Giving back to those who raised me
Making me a better person.

Wife and mother,
Keeper of schedules,
Protector and guardian
A rock in times of need
They are the center of my world.

These things that I love,
They make me complete,
Give me purpose in this world,
Cement my identity-
I am whole and unashamed.

Deeply Rooted

Character is deeply rooted within-
Tangling in the very fabric of life.
It is hard to say herein,
When through it all we deal with strife.

Be upstanding and do what is right,
So that I can look in the mirror-
When I close my eyes at the end of the
night
I hold that feeling to me dearer.

Honesty is a value we treasure
Confidence in what you say and do,
Seeing a genuine smile gives me such
pleasure-
It makes it so easy to say "I love you".

Make them smile, or make them cry
Values are also deeply rooted in me,
I am unfailingly honest, I cannot lie.
Good girl or bad, which shall I be?

Who I am can change day to day,
Make a stand against violence,

Encourage others to join in the fray-
Because we cannot stand in silence.

Be brave, be caring, be unfailingly you,
Deeply rooted values are what we do.

"Winter Day"

Snow falls lightly on
    Covering footsteps quietly
    As I walk, all alone

"Red"

Flame of a aromatic cigar,
Rolled tight by gnarled hands.
Fire trucks rush to put out the flames,
Of a blaze at once destructive and hypnotic.
Heat, the mercury begins to climb,
Burning tender skin.
Passion flares, red-hot,
Lips meet in a searing kiss.
Love blinds you,
Coloring the world around you.
Betrayal stings,
Carving words of hate in your heart.
Blood boils,
an angry scream ripped from the throat.
Pain rips through you,
Blood flows in rivers down your arms.
Heart open, nerves exposed,
Raw, pulsing with emotion and need.

"Puzzle Pieces"

We are merely pieces
In the jigsaw puzzle of life.
Rounded corners, indents,
Square edges carved through strife.

We go through our lives looking for matches,
Pieces that can fit into you seamlessly.
How do the colors match up?
Looking for matches endlessly.

I am a center piece,
Cool colors and several indents,
Looking for love and acceptance,
Wondering if our fit is meant.

When we join together,
A picture begins to emerge.
Colors and feelings,
Emotions begin to surge.

Uh oh, there's a piece
That doesn't quite fit,
What should we do
With this little misfit?

Do we shave off the edges,
Smooth it into a pleasing shape?
Or let it alone,
And watch with mouths agape?

Perhaps the misfit
Really does belong,
When we flip it around
It fit all along.

The image of our puzzle
Begins to emerge
And layer upon layer,
Our lives also merge.

"I Said"

It was a hot summer night,
Music thrummed through the air,
Everyone was swaying to the beat.

People packed in like sardines
To the nightclub on the strip,
Flesh gleaming with sweat.

Dark, hungry eyes
Followed my progress
Through the dizzying array of dancers.

I ordered a drink,
Vodka with cranberry juice-
Hoping to quench my thirst.

Before I could pay,
A hand snaked in front
Of me and handed him a twenty.

Turned and looked into a brooding face,
Eyes that roamed me hungrily,
"Thank you," I said.

He smiled, shark like teeth,
Overpowering cologne,
“Want to Dance?”

“I’d like that,” I said.
Bodies moving,
Rough hands on my hips.

“Let me drive you home,”
Said with a smile,
“Okay,” I said.

The side of the road,
Pawing at my skin-
“No,” I said.

He didn’t listen,
Now I am a statistic.

"Mistakes"

Mistakes, I've made a few-
I joke and say I wore polyester and spats
In my high school years-
Marching band.
But I learned there too.

I learned to be a friend,
A listener,
I had my first date-
Though, to be fair, it was a bust.

I never went to a college party-
Didn't want to fake that I drank,
Didn't want to listen to awful music,
Didn't want to be a wallflower.

Learned from that too-
Learned that life isn't about parties
And drinking and smoking,
But about friendship and relationships
And about responsibility.

Got engaged too young,
That all fell apart.
Walking, crying down Main St.
Really taught me a lot.

Taught me to be resilient,
To not give away my heart
Too easily to someone who
Didn't deserve it.

Got credit cards in college-
quickly learned that mistake.
Spending is fun,
But you have to pay that back,
Eventually.

Credit still recovering,
But I learned to be smarter,
Have a savings account
In case of a rainy day.
I've trusted the wrong people,
Been burned there too.
Lost loves, friends, and
Family too.
Hard to overcome some mistakes.

Spoke my mind,
Stood up for what I believed in,
Made a couple mistakes.
Life is about growing, or so they say.

Mistakes shape us,
They are the lines we color outside,
The wrong chord in a beautiful song,
They teach us invaluable lessons.

We are not defined by our mistakes,
But we need to learn from them
To grow and become more,
On the traumas of our pasts,
We need to close that door.

"Ten Questions for Shakespeare"

1. Did you ever really love her?
   Your long-suffering wife,
   Did you even consider
   Her feelings at all?

2. Why abandon your family?
   Moving to London,
   Becoming an actor
   Was not cool to do.
   Did you not miss them at all?
   Your beautiful children,
   Their smiles and antics.

3. Did you actually write all of your work?
   I want to believe it,
   To recognize your genius
   And incredible talent.
   Choosing just the right words
   To convey your meaning.

4. Why did you not act more on stage?
   Taking the small roles,
   Playing a ghost.
   Why not rule the stage?

Strut around proudly,
Show off your talent.

5. What do you consider your pinnacle work?
King Lear a father's sadness-
Macbeth a jealous nobleman-
I rather think the greatest work
Is that of Hamlet- the damned prince.

6. Who is the Dark Lady?
A streetwalker,
Her beauty is so clear,
Yet you are vague about her.
A friend's wife, a lady of the court,
Her identity is still not known.
Perhaps she was a conglomerate of several
Women that you knew….

7. How did Hamnet's death affect you?
Did you rave at the injustice,
The pointlessness of it all.
Just a boy, not yet a man,
Your line died with him.
You wrote a play about a fatherless son,
Did a childless father cut too close?

8. Why did you retire?
Were you tired of the daily grind,
Making a living with quill and parchment,
Did the greasepaint leave lasting marks,
Did you have too many lines stepped on
By inferior actors
Or were you just ready to go home?

9. Were your last years peaceful?
Did you enjoy those final years,
Spend time with your daughters,
Read books with your wife by the fireside.
Did you walk the paths in Stratford,
Soak in the natural beauty of the countryside.

10. Why the inscription on your tomb?
Were you really afraid of grave robbers,
Men who skulk in the shadows
Stealing from the dead.
Did you wish to remain alone, undisturbed?
A solitary man in life and in death.
An unparalleled genius.

"Chris"

It's funny, really,
how a chance encounter
can change your life.

I met you so long ago,
we shared only a few
real hours together.

Dancing in the gloomy light
from the garage's windows
"Every Rose Has Its Thorn".

That night changed everything-
I found a true friend,
a rock on which I could lean.

I became a rock for you,
to listen to your fears,
to try and dry the tears.

I'd never really thought about
The idea of mental illness-
I didn't see how broken you were.

When we lost you,
I would have never guessed
How the demons plagued you.

You gave up you life,
So hurt by others,
Leaving behind pain and sadness.

Your beautiful soul,
Your incredible talent,
Silenced forever with the blade of a knife.

Saying goodbye was so hard,
I'd never lost someone I'd loved,
you were barely seventeen.

My whole world changed,
I confronted darkness through your death
And I reached for the light.

Your death left a void,
A yawning hole in my heart,
A forever missing piece.

To this day, I know you are here,
When our song plays on the radio,
My guardian angel, keeping watch.

"Ocean"

I am the daughter of Poseidon,
The sand and the sea, two worlds colliding,
My heart beats in time with the tide,
Under the waves, on a dolphin I ride.

The sirens sing a love song
That calls me home all along
I hear my father's voice inside my head,
Through the channels and depths I am led.

Being near the ocean is where I am free,
Wild, untamed, beautifully me,
Come join me in the underwater revelry,
There is nowhere else I'd rather be.

In the eyes of a great white shark,
I see the intelligence and cunning spark,
It is something I have never seen hence,
The deep unending currents of violence.

Upon the crabs I like to spy,
Sneaking up to make them cry,
Their little claws they like to flaunt
Even though they are pretty gaunt.

Being near the ocean is where I am free,
Wild, untamed, beautifully me,
Come join me in the underwater revelry,
There is nowhere else I'd rather be.

Song of the ocean will call me home,
No matter where on earth I choose to roam,
It calls to me in the dusky gloaming,
In the surf, so innocently foaming.

When at the shore I finally arrive,
It is there where I begin to feel alive,
Into the ocean I dive and play,
Smiling and happy at the end of the day.
Being near the ocean is where I am free,
Wild, untamed, beautifully me,
Come, join me in the underwater revelry,
There is nowhere else I'd rather be.

"Peace"

Snowy day outside
Walking in the world of of white
Quiet and calm mind

"Work Space"

I have an office in the house,
It is often quieter than a mouse,
From my chair I can look out the window,
And see the action in my yard below.

My desk is messy and full of stuff,
From the cigar by my side I may occasionally
puff,
A red mini fridge holds my soda,
And on my shelf, watching, is my stuffed baby
Yoda.

On my wall a plaque proclaiming "Roll Tide,"
And paintings I made of oceans wide.
This space is my blessed sanctuary,
I come here when I am stressed or wary.

My macbook is where I keep my writing,
And often a candle I find myself lighting.
Keeping away the dreaded writer's block,
Often I yell, for my children don't knock.

I very often grade quizzes and tests,
In many cases, my students do their best.
I write poems, stories, and sometimes even lists,
Bits and pieces and sometimes just the gist.

My workspace is cluttered, but it seems to me,
That I know where everything is or might be.
While it might not make any real sense to you,
To me it’s as clear as the ocean blue.

"Josh"

We had quite the auspicious meeting,
I talked to Chris without even acknowledging
you,
Dressed in my Papa's gear, smeared with sauce,
You didn't even blink- just asked him who I
was.
Chris told you no- that I was a good girl.
But that didn't stop you from coming around,
Sitting at Papa's staring through the crowd.
Our first date was watching a movie- my choice,
"Lady and the Tramp" with popcorn- your
choice.
We knew very quickly that we were meant to be,
Moved in together, and even got a pug.

Ups and downs, highs and lows,
We've been there, done that.
Got married, had kids, the usual track,
Raising babies into people took a bit of luck.
Friends have come, and friends have gone,
Always, we have had each other.
We laugh, we cry, we play together,
Dancing, axes, paintball, breweries,
Wineries, traveling, or just hanging out.

When the days get longer, we sit outside,
Enjoying the home we have created,
A piece of paradise we made.
When troubles come, we face them as one,
Hands held tightly, knowing we have each others' backs.
Almost twenty five years together,
And a lifetime more to go.

Together,
We will face any challenges,
We will get through each day,
We face illness, death and destruction,
We rise up and conquer,
Together.

"Chances"

How many chances are we expected to give?
How many ways can we hurt each other?
You have chances to make little mistakes,
Things that don't have dire consequences.
When you lie, those cuts are shallow,
When you cheat, those cuts run deep.

My love for you allows for chances,
Because no one is perfect all the time.
We all have bad days, get headaches,
Think that we aren't good enough.
There are rules that everyone should follow,
The currents of love run true and deep.

Chances are opportunities,
A way to atone,
To realize you are wrong,
To make a positive change.
Chances are words you must swallow
So that over the crevasse between us you leap.

Come to me,
Give me your honesty and heart,
Swear that this is the last time,
You won't lie again,

Don't let your words sound fake and hollow,
Or out the door your lies I will sweep.

I don't need much,
Just your truth and your love,
To give me the edge in life.
You and I have been through so much,
Our love flutters like the tiny sparrow
Whose hope is ours to forever keep.

"Things I've Lost"

Our lives are quite often full,
We don't even realize that we lose little things
Every day.
We lose memories,
How did grandma take her coffee?
What was grandpa's favorite song?
Little things that we don't even realize.

We lose images,
Did Pep's eyes twinkle when he laughed?
Did Meme always live in her chair?
Was my great grandpa six feet tall?
Pull out the photos, examine them carefully.
Find the clues there for me to see.

We lose sounds;
The sound of crickets chirping while we danced,
The sound of my grandpa's whistling,
The sound of popcorn in the stovetop popper
While waiting for the Bruins game to start.

I have lost friends,
Chris, Jason, Patrick, and Matt,
To suicide- the darkness swallowed their lights.
I have lost family,

Many to the disease of Cancer,
Others to old age.
Losing people I love can destroy
Pieces of my heart with every death.

I have lost so much in life,
Said goodbye too early,
Missed out on so many conversations.
I wish I'd know that I'd lose them,
So I could have made other choices.
I didn't want to stand by and watch,
Wanted to be able to change things.

I have lost faith in humanity,
Watching people commit acts of violence,
Witnessing murders, police brutality and war.
How can we do these things to ourselves?

We can only hope for the best,
To do our jobs every day,
To make the most of our lives
And build a brighter future.

"Magic"

There is magic in the winter landscape,
When snow covers the sleeping land,
Standing in the snow, mouth agape,
Trying to catch a snowflake in your hand.

There is magic sitting in front of a roaring fire,
Listening to songs on vinyl,
Vocals and instrumentals that inspire
Crackling embers, the fire dying, final.

There is magic in your warm embrace,
Safe from all that could harm me,
Your smile causes my heart to race,
There is nowhere else I'd rather be.

There is magic in our spoken words,
The lilting cadence of each individual voice,
They can cut us through, cleanly, like swords,
Leaving us with not a single choice.

There is magic in the children we created,
Our love, our characters, our united selves,
Living in the home we provided,
Deep into their hearts they often delve.

There is magic in our love, its true,
For there is no one else I would stand beside,
Who gives me the attention and pride I am due,
With you, into Hell, I would willingly ride.

"Words That Make Me Smile"

Cacophony- a harsh, discordant sound-
I always associate with children playing,
Sauciness- pert attitude, irreverent-
I love to say, "I feel saucy today!"
Melodious- sweet sounds, with harmony-
something my voice just can never be.
Unrequited- not returned-
sometimes the best kind of love, because it
means there is another.
loquacious- talkative, chattering-
here I see little girls, telling secrets at a
sleepover,
Confusticated- borrowed from Tolkien, meaning
confused-
one of my favorite lines from The Hobbit

None of these are made up words,
they all are from our beautiful language,
words that sound so pretty-
gossamer, imbue, effervescent, demure,
lassitude, malaise, subterfuge and woebegone.

We need to use these words more,
we need that poetry to brighten our otherwise
drab days,
words have power, and you need to wield them
with majestic, opulent splendour,
these enthralling, stupendous, glorious words,
bring hope and beauty to us.

Consider the precious swell of a baby bump,
the dazzling radiance of brilliant gemstone,
the bewitching and tantalizing song of Sirens,
imagine being flabbergasted by the shenanigans
of youth,
lollygagging behind the group to canoodle.
Your persnickety ways causing a kerfuffle,
and heavens to betsy- perhaps a brouhaha,
it all leaves others gobsmacked and flummoxed.

"The End"

This sounds so final- the end-
it is but a mere stop along the journey,
a weigh station at which we unload some of our
cares,
allowing us room to onboard others.

Move forward confidently,
with head held high and shoulders straight,
looking at each comer straight in the eye,
meet the haughty gazes with your own steely
one.

For this end is but momentary,
a taking stock of our lives.
This end is just a blip in the cosmic highway,
I plan on exploding, a firework of light.

Dazzling and brilliant I will bring you joy,
and hope that in my words you have found
some comfort, some hope, and maybe desire
to converse in this language of ours.

To love.

www.ingramcontent.com/pod-product-compliance
Lightning Source LLC
Chambersburg PA
CBHW051744130826
49812CB00033B/1002
9789357440912